A GENTLEMAN PENS A NOTE

JOHN BRIDGES

BRYAN CURTIS

Rutledge Hill Press™
Nashville, Tennessee

A Division of Thomas Nelson, Inc.
www.ThomasNelson.com

To Iris and Mike Buhl,
as ever—duly noted
—J.B.

To Larry Stone,
for all the doors you've opened for me
—B.C.

Published by Rutledge Hill Press, a Division of Thomas Nelson, Inc., P.O. Box 141000, Nashville, Tennessee 37214.

Library of Congress Cataloging-in-Publication Data

Bridges, John, 1950–
  A gentleman pens a note / John Bridges, Bryan Curtis.
     p. cm.
  ISBN 1-4016-0109-X
  1. Etiquette for men. 2. Letter-writing. I. Curtis, Bryan. II. Title.
  BJ1601.B757 2003
  395.4—dc21   2003004670

Printed in the United States of America
03 04 05 06 07 — 5 4 3 2

INTRODUCTION

Saying "I'm sorry" or "thank you" should be the simplest task in the world, but it is not. Instead it is one of the most fearsome challenges faced by gentlemen in today's complex, less-than-mannerly, less-than-thoughtful society.

A gentleman will be greatly assisted, however, by remembering a few rules that always remain the same. It is never wrong to write a note, either on good cardstock or via e-mail. It is never wrong to say, via any form of communication, "Congratulations to you," "Sorry about the death of your mother," "Best wishes on your upcoming nuptials," "Wasn't that a *great* party?" or "I really look forward to using my new multi-pop-up toaster."

Still, far too often a man views the writing of a thank-you note, a sympathy note, or a note of congratulation as a woeful obligation. He might better consider his thank-you note as the completion of a lovely evening, or even a continuance of a wonderfully fulfilling experience. Similarly, his sympathy note can well be seen as his expression of concern for a close friend who is grieving, or his acknowledgment of the death of a personal mentor, a beloved friend, a civic leader, or even a benefactor or volunteer who has made the world a better place.

His challenge is always to find the right words—and to identify the moments when he should write them. He always tries to write a note that will not embarrass him, but deep in his heart he knows that, if he thinks to write any note at all, he has already made it clear that he knows what kindness, consideration, and gratitude are all about.

This volume reminds a gentleman that the moment he feels the urge to write a note about anything is the moment when he should pick up his pen.

When a gentleman writes a note,
he keeps it simple.

A gentleman does not consider thank-you
notes, congratulatory notes, or sympathy notes
a burden. Instead he considers each note a tiny,
inexpensive tribute to a person whom he
respects, to whom he is grateful, or whose
company he enjoys.

A gentleman knows that note writing is almost a lost art. Even by sending the simplest thank-you, he knows that he has separated himself from the non-note-writing throng.

A gentleman is lucky if his parents forced him to write thank-you notes for presents received for his sixth birthday—or even earlier.

A gentleman knows that, even if he did not have such parents, it is never too late to learn.

A gentleman provides his own children, and other children of his acquaintance, with their own stationery and cards for use in social correspondence. He knows that they will never develop ladylike or gentlemanly habits if they lack the proper tools.

If a gentleman wants the young people in his life to grow up writing thank-you notes, he sets a good example by sending notes to them as soon as they can read, thanking them for their gifts and kindnesses to him.

A gentleman writes as clearly as he can.

On the other hand, a gentleman does
not fret about the quality of his penmanship.

A gentleman knows that a thank-you note
written in a particularly gnarly hand can afford
its recipient endless hours of amusement.

If a gentleman's handwriting is absolutely indecipherable, he may resort to his word processor.

A gentleman always signs his notes by hand, even if he must append his typewritten name underneath his signature so as not to leave his correspondent in a quandary.

If a gentleman is unsure of the spelling of any word, he looks it up in a dictionary.

Before a gentleman puts any letter or note in the mail, he reads it over at least once, checking for any omissions or errors that may have been made in the heat, or merriment, of the moment.

A gentleman always makes sure to attach the necessary postage to his correspondence. Otherwise he has wasted his own good time and created an unnecessary inconvenience for the person to whom he is writing.

A gentleman does not resort to the aid of a thesaurus when he writes a personal note. He knows that he is better off using the same simple word twice than misusing a more unusual word in the hope of breaking the monotony.

When writing a sympathy note, a gentleman does not resort to euphemisms that avoid the simple fact of mortality. He resists referring to the dead person's "passing." Neither does he lament the fact that the deceased has "left us" or "departed." A gentleman is better advised simply to say, "I am sorry to learn about Larry's death."

If a gentleman does not have any high-quality stationery on hand, he feels perfectly comfortable using any clean, unornamented, unruled paper that is available.

When it comes to selecting his own stationery, a gentleman knows that simplicity is always in unassailable good taste.

A gentleman never uses his business stationery or his business cards for personal correspondence.

If a gentleman expects to send handwritten notes with any degree of frequency, he equips himself with pens (either classic fountain pens or good-quality disposable pens) with black or blue-black ink.

A gentleman knows that pen and ink and personal stationery are not appropriate for some correspondence. When he must write to a creditor or a debtor, or when he submits an application to a potential employer, he uses his computer or, if he still owns such a thing, his typewriter.

A gentleman shies away from using cards with messages such as "Thank You," "Congratulations," or "In Sympathy" already imprinted on the cover. He knows that those words will mean a great deal more written in his own hand than gold-embossed by a printer.

When sending a thank-you note for a dinner party that is hosted by a husband and wife, or by any man-and-woman team, a gentleman traditionally directs his note to his hostess rather than his host. If he has been a guest of Jim and Joe, or Mimsey and Martha, however, he directs his note to both hosts or hostesses.

When saying thank you for a gift or for a dinner or cocktail party, a gentleman feels no need to promise to reciprocate.

When saying thank you for a gift or for having been entertained in a particularly generous way, a gentleman never mentions the cost of the present or the size of the dinner tab.

When declining an invitation, a gentleman need not offer a lengthy explanation for his inability to accept the kindness of his host or hostess. He is perfectly correct simply to say, "I have another engagement."

A gentleman knows that saying thank you is the surest means of being invited again. Nevertheless, when he writes his thank-you notes, his motivation is never so self-serving.

A gentleman does not expect any response when he sends a thank-you note (or even a thank-you gift).

When a gentleman receives a thank-you note, he does not send a reply. He may, however, choose to say at some appropriate encounter, "I received your very kind note. You were nice to send it."

When to Write a Note

A gentleman knows that a handwritten note is never inappropriate, whether he is responding to an invitation, saying thank you for a lovely evening, expressing sympathy, or extending his congratulations to newlyweds or to the parents of a new baby.

Even if he has already conveyed his thanks (or congratulations or condolences) by phone or by e-mail, a gentleman still relishes the chance to put his thoughts in writing, even if his handwriting is well nigh indecipherable.

He does his best to post his note as promptly as possible, but he knows that even an overdue note is better than no note at all.

Excuses A Gentleman Never Uses
for Not Writing a Note

My handwriting is miserable.

I didn't have the right paper.

I didn't know what to say.

I've waited too long now.

If I sit down to write a note now,
it's the only thing I'll get done tonight.

These folks are so busy,
they won't even know who I am.

THANK-YOU NOTES

A gentleman never finds it burdensome to say thank you for a gift or for a good time. He attempts to send his thanks as swiftly as possible. (If he is particularly clever, he writes his thank-you note immediately upon returning from the party for which he is grateful, no matter how late he gets home in the evening—or morning.) He knows, however, that it is almost impossible for a thank-you note to be *too* late. He feels no guilt (well, *almost* no guilt) in sending a thank-you note weeks, months, or even a year after the fact, provided he knows how to word the note in the most diplomatic manner he can manage.

In writing a thank-you note, even for a gift he did not particularly appreciate or a party he did not especially enjoy, a gentleman always handles himself gracefully by making some specific mention of the gift itself or of some aspect of the party. He need not grow effusive in his appreciation. His only responsibility is to say that he appreciates the thoughtfulness of the person who gave him the gift or was his host or hostess.

A gentleman need not write a thank-you note for a bottle of wine or a holiday ornament brought along as a "host gift" by a guest at a party hosted by the gentleman himself. If he has received his gift as part of a holiday gift exchange among friends, he writes a quick note expressing his gratitude, not so much for the gift itself as for the friend's thoughtfulness. He also makes sure to mention how he plans to use it or how it fits into his life.

A gentleman sincerely appreciates any gift that comes his way. Sometimes, however, he receives a gift that is not precisely the one he would choose. For example, he may receive a windbreaker emblazoned with the logo of a football team he does not support. He may receive a set of cocktail glasses he never intends to use. He may receive a book that he never intends to read. He may receive a tie that he finds insulting, even as a gift. Still, he understands that the gift is intended as a compliment, and he treats it as such.

Basing his judgment upon the relative formality of an occasion he has attended, the nature of the gift he has received, or the importance of a kindness done for him, a gentleman may choose to write his thank-you note on his very best stationery or correspondence card, or he may choose to dash off a few words on the back of an attractive or amusing postcard.

In writing a thank-you note, more than in any other type of correspondence, a gentleman attempts to avoid any hint of stuffiness. He attempts, instead, to convey the sense of joy that he felt when the gift was offered and received.

A Thank-You Note for a
Gift Happily Received

Dear Jesse,

You know how much I love good, simple wine glasses.
When I opened your package the other night, I was
reminded of your good taste and your unfailing generosity.
Very soon, when I use these glasses, I intend to make a
toast to you.

Sincerely,
Phil

A Gentleman Does Not Write:

"Who knew you had such good taste?"

A Thank-You Note for a Gift That You Really Don't Care For

Dear Gene and Ginger,

How could you have known that I'm thinking about taking golf lessons? Your set of monogrammed tees will be a real inspiration to me as I head for the course. Please know that I'm going to save them until I won't do them too much damage.

Thank you so much for being part of my birthday party.

Sincerely,
Granger

A Gentleman Does Not Write:

"Thanks. It's certainly not anything I'd ever have
thought of buying for myself."

A Thank-You Note for a Holiday Gift When a Gentleman Has Not Given a Gift in Return

My Dear Gladys,

It was such a surprise to see you on my doorstep the day before Christmas, and you were so kind to give me the swim goggles. I'm looking forward to wearing them on my trip to Bali. It was so good of you to think of me in this way.

Wish we could see each other more often. Let's try to rectify that in the New Year.

I hope your holidays were great. Just seeing you made mine special.

Much love,
Rollo

A Gentleman Does Not Write:

"I wish I'd known you were getting
me something."

A Thank-You Note for an At-Home Dinner Party

Dear Mary Sue,

Saturday night's dinner party was a truly lovely occasion. You always manage to attract such an interesting mix of people, and the dinner was a veritable feast. I particularly love white chocolate, so the dessert almost made me shout for joy.

Thanks, too, for seating me next to Kathy. I loved getting to hear about her work with songwriters, and as it turns out, we're both from Kentucky.

Only you could make this kind of evening happen.

All my best,
Russ

A Gentleman Does Not Write:

"I'm sure the food was delicious—
I should have told you I'm allergic to shellfish."

A Thank-You Note for Dinner at a Restaurant

Dear Oscar,

You were great to include me in dinner last night at The Beaver's Paw. I had read so many great reviews of the place—both the food and the service.

Last night certainly lived up to my every expectation. In fact, The Paw may now be on my really short list of favorite bistros in town.

It's always a pleasure to be in your company. You really are one of the best hosts on the planet.

Thanks for a wonderful, memorable evening.

All my best,
Boris

A Gentleman Does Not Write:

"For such an inexpensive place,
the food was pretty good."

A Thank-You Note for a Dinner Party That Did Not Go So Well

Dear Jessica,

It's always a pleasure to be in your presence, even when the gas jets aren't working. You were so smart to go ahead and bring in the pizza. Sitting around the living room, even with our overcoats on, we had the greatest time trying to distinguish the pepperoni from the veggie sausage.

With the help of Jack's wine cellar, we certainly persevered.

You are a trouper. But then, wasn't it fun to discover what troupers all of us can be—when we're having a really wonderful time.

> Thanks for a bold,
> adventurous evening,
> Alfred

A Gentleman Does Not Write:

"I guess you'll remember to
pay the gas bill next time."

A Thank-You Note for a Gift Written Long After the Fact

Dear Tracey and Hank,

This very morning I was drinking my cocoa from one of the funny "Kats R Kurious" mugs you gave me last Hanukkah. I still remember what fun I had just opening the package. Trust me, every time I use one of them—especially the one with the cat attempting to get the fireman down from the tree—I still laugh out loud.

Thanks for giving me such continuing pleasure.

Hope all is well with you and the boys.

Sincerely,
Izzy

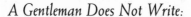

A Gentleman Does Not Write:

"I'm so sorry this note is so late. I must
be getting Alzheimer's."

A Thank-You Note for a Dinner Party Written Long After the Fact

Dear Brendan,

Yesterday while I was out for my midday run, I passed Kelly's Pub, where I could already smell the hickory smoke from the grill. Just that experience took me back to your cookout on Labor Day, and all the fun of it came back to me—especially your own perfectly smoked ribs.

Thanks for giving me such a great memory.

Best wishes,
Tom

A Gentleman Does Not Write:

"You'll have to forgive me,
but I have been too busy to write."

A Thank-You Note After Being a House Guest

Dear Loretta and Ron,

What fun it was getting to spend time with you in your beautiful condo this past weekend. It was great to wake up every morning and smell that fresh coffee brewing.

You were so kind to introduce me to your friends and to show me the sights in Bankersville. The new RollerDome is a marvel.

Best of all, however, was the time we had to relax and enjoy one another's company.

I hope you'll come visit Rockwart sometime soon. Say hi to the puppies for me.

Thanks so much,
Joe

A Gentleman Does Not Write:

"Your home was so clean—
you must have hired a maid
before I arrived."

A Thank-You Note for an Extraordinary Kindness

Dear Johnny,

You were so noble to help me through a tough time last week while I was stuck without a car. Those were especially busy days for me, and I don't know exactly what I would have done if you hadn't been so generous in letting me borrow the Honda.

Please know how much I appreciate your readiness to help a guy through a tough spot. Now that the Bentley's back up and running, let's go have a drink some time soon. I'll give you a buzz.

All my thanks.

Sincerely,
Ben

A Gentleman Does Not Write:

"Here's ten dollars for the gas
I used. You can check the mileage
if you want to."

A Thank-You Note for a Job Interview

Dear Ms. Longstray:

It was a pleasure to meet with you this afternoon. I appreciated the chance to learn more about Longstray and Bailey. I was especially interested to hear about your expansion in the fields of foliage retrieval and mulch creation.

Everything I heard today certainly reaffirms my thinking that the Advertising Division of Longstray and Bailey is a place where I could make a real contribution, given my experience and my personal commitment to recycling.

I look forward to continuing our conversation and will stay in touch with Ms. Pebbly in Human Resources.

Thanks so much for your time and your insights.

Sincerely yours,
Albert Josenblick

[*Although Albert's letter is a business letter, it is a personal letter too. Since his thank-you letter must look as professional and businesslike as possible, it should be typewritten. A handwritten note is also acceptable, but it must be written on a gentleman's personal stationery or on a clean sheet of high-quality writing paper, with his return address and phone number clearly indicated at the top of the page. When applying for a new job, a gentleman never uses his current employer's stationery—or postage. To do so might lead his potential employer to question the gentleman's integrity, not to mention his business ethics.*]

A Gentleman Does Not Write:

"I really want this job, and—assuming you can pay me what I'm worth—I will probably take it."

When Not to Write a Note

There are very rare instances when a gentleman may find it permissible, or even wise, *not* to write a note.

For example, he does not write a thank-you note for dinner parties or other occasions that are fund-raisers, either for charity or for political causes. Because he was present as a result of having written a check, he was in a very real way helping to throw the party. Therefore, no thank-you is required. (On the other hand, if an event has been particularly well produced, he may wish to dash off a congratulatory note to the people who made it happen.)

Neither does he feel driven to write a note for an everyday kindness, such as a friend's offering to buy him a soda, giving him a ride to the airport, or proofreading his section of the office annual report. Because there is really no such thing as an "everyday" kindness, however, a gentleman still makes a point of saying thank you and offering to return the favor when his help is needed.

What is more, a gentleman may find himself in situations where he would just as soon leave no written record of the experience. Confronted with an unfair accusation of rudeness, unfaithfulness, or unfairness, for example, he is best advised not to put his response (much less his emotions) on paper. He is best advised to handle such unpleasant situations in person, not even by means of telephone or (even worse) answering machine. He may discover far too late that his words have been recorded, making them every bit as problematic as if he'd written them down in his best blue-black ink.

In extremely difficult or complex situations, a gentleman lets his attorney do the writing.

A Gentleman and His E-mail

A gentleman's e-mail can prove highly useful in personal correspondence, provided the gentleman uses it with discretion.

He may use his e-mail to respond to any informal invitation or to send a brief thank-you for a friend's kindness. He may even send out via e-mail an invitation for cocktails or a casual dinner. This means of communication is *only* appropriate, however, in situations where a phone call might accomplish the same task.

Upon hearing of the birth of a new baby, a friend's new job, or even the death of a friend's loved one or close relation, a gentleman may send an e-mail, notifying his friend that he has heard the news. In every case, however, he immediately follows up with a handwritten note. A gentleman never sends an e-mail in response to a formal invitation.

SYMPATHY NOTES,
NOTES OF CONCERN,
AND RESPONSES TO THEM

A gentleman knows that, in times of bereavement and trouble, the most honest, direct words are the best words possible. If he has been well acquainted with the person who has died, his note includes some mention of that person's good attributes or a remembrance of the person's kind treatment of the gentleman himself. ("I remember how welcoming your mother was, Jim, every time we'd come home, all covered in mud, after the football games in the park.")

On the other hand, if he did not actually know the deceased person, a gentleman may express his sympathies directly to his friend, saying, "Jim, I have heard about your mother's death. Please know that you are in my thoughts."

A gentleman may feel confident in writing a sympathy note upon the death of any good friend, close coworker, or acquaintance. He may also feel comfortable in expressing his sympathy to any friend or coworker who has lost a relative, a close friend, or even a cherished pet.

In such situations he need not be too specific in his condolences. Instead he is wise to focus on his relationship with his friend or coworker: "I've heard about Polly's death. I know she meant a great deal to you. Please know you are in my thoughts."

In some instances a gentleman may wish to extend condolences to several family members who do not live in the same household. In such cases, he may choose to write a number of notes, all of them virtually identical, one to each of his friends. He is better advised, however, to send one well-worded note to one of the bereaved, adding at the end of the note, "I hope you will share my thoughts with Jim, Jack, Suzy, and Sam. I am thinking of you all at this time."

If a gentleman is a praying person, he may replace "you are in my thoughts" with "you are in my prayers."

A bereaved gentleman realizes that not only flowers sent in a time of concern, but also cards and kind words, should be acknowledged with a short note. This note does not have to be lengthy because a gentleman may have hundreds of such notes to write. A few short words are all that is required to let someone know that his or her gesture was sincerely appreciated.

A Sympathy Note to a Close Friend upon the Death of a Spouse or Life Partner

Dear Marianne,

I've just learned about Jim's death. It's hard for me to know what to say at this moment, but I do know that I remember all the great times we spent together (the two of you, with Ginny and me). He was generous of spirit, in all things. I never remember him refusing to try any new adventure.

Ginny and I have always admired the warmth and camaraderie of your relationship. I know you will miss him. So will Ginny. And so will I.

Please know that you are in our thoughts.

Sincerely,
Ted

A Gentleman Does Not Write:

"I know exactly what you are going through.
When I lost Sally . . ."

A Sympathy Note upon the Death of a Business Acquaintance or the Death of a Coworker's Relative

Dear Tom (or Mr. Gruston),

Just today Sibbley Clark told me about Jennifer's death [or "about the death of Mrs. Gruston"]. Although I did not know her well, I do know something about her presence in the business community and her many good works as a community volunteer. Here in the office, it always made me particularly happy to hear about your shared devotion to your family.

Please know that my thoughts ["and Mary Sue's," if applicable] are with you at this time.

Sincerely,
Otto [or "Otto Bailey"]

A Gentleman Does Not Write:

"It just goes to show you—we never know when
we will be taken from this earth."

A Sympathy Note to a Friend
or Coworker upon the
Death of a Close Friend

Dear Harry,

I know how much Lester meant to you as a friend. I always enjoyed hearing you talk about your great times on your camping trips. Just listening to those stories, I got the sense that he was a fun guy and a really special person to you.

Just wanted you to know that I was thinking about you.

Sincerely,
Preston

A Gentleman Does Not Write:

"I know this is a hard time for you, but don't
let this get you down."

A Sympathy Note upon the
Death of a Child

Dear Esther and Eric,

The news of Jessica's death fills me with great sadness. I have always admired your family for its closeness and the warmth you have so clearly shared.

Please know that you are in my thoughts.

Sincerely,
Houston

A Gentleman Does Not Write:

"It should give you some comfort to know
that Jessica is in heaven."

A Sympathy Note upon the Death of an Infant or a Miscarriage

Dear Patty and Paul,

I have just heard of your loss. I will not attempt to find words to express my sadness, since there are no words that can handle this moment in anybody's life.

Please know, however, that I am thinking of you.

Sincerely,
Mike

A Gentleman Does Not Write:

"If there is anything I can do for you,
please let me know."

A Sympathy Note to a Friend or Coworker upon the Death of a Beloved Pet

Dear Hallie,

I was really sad to learn about Mr. Bibbs's death. I know that he was one of your best pals, always accepting and ready to have fun.

As he got on in age, I truly admired the way you gave him the care and loving comfort that seemed right, in appreciation of the joy he had brought into your life.

Sincerely,
Barton

A Gentleman Does Not Write:

"You must have been expecting this—
Mr. Bibbs was pretty old for a cat."

A Response to a Sympathy Note

Dear Otto,

Your kind words were a great comfort in the wake of Maggie's death. These are tough times, but your support and concern are a true source of strength.

Thank you so much for lending your support in this special way.

Sincerely,
Tom Gruston

A Gentleman Does Not Write:

"The bright side of this is that I now know
how many people care for me."

A Note of Concern for a
Friend's Health

Dear Edward,

I have heard the news about your diagnosis. There is no reason that this disease chooses to strike one person rather than another. You are, however, a brave, strong-willed fellow, and you have an army of friends to stick with you through the coming days.

Please know how honored I am to be one of that army.

You are in my thoughts.

Sincerely,
Peter

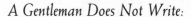

A Gentleman Does Not Write:

"I hope you will finally begin taking care of
yourself—I don't want to lose you."

A Note of Concern for the Loss of a Job

Dear Ursula,

Jack told me today that you are no longer with Pacific Packaging. I know how much you enjoyed working for them, and I know how devoted you were to the company.

As you move toward your next adventure, please know that I, like so many others, will want to hear about your progress. Please know that we're there to support you.

I'll call you in the next few days, and we'll grab some lunch. Okay?

I know this is probably a tough time. You are in my thoughts.

Sincerely,
Carlos

A Gentleman Does Not Write:

"If there is anything I can do for you—
short of a loan—let me know."

A NOTE OF CONCERN AT THE BREAKUP
OF A RELATIONSHIP

Dear Chuck,

I'm so sorry to hear about you and Debra. I value you both as friends, and I regret that things are not working out. I know you both did your best to make your relationship work.

This is a difficult time, I'm sure, but I hope you'll let me and the rest of your friends provide the support that we're ready to offer.

I'll be in touch sometime later this week. Maybe we can grab a drink or shoot some hoops.

Sincerely,
Dennis

A Gentleman Does Not Write:

"I must admit—you stuck it out longer than
I would have. I have got the perfect girl for you
to meet. Just give me the word and
I'll introduce you."

A Response to a Card or Letter of Concern

Dear Peter,

I hope you know how your kind words encouraged me during my stay in the hospital. The surgery hit me with a wallop that I hadn't expected, so I really valued the support of thoughtful friends like you.

Now that I'm back up and running—almost at full speed— I look forward to seeing you in the very near future.

Many, many thanks.

Sincerely,
Edward

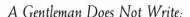

A Gentleman Does Not Write:

"I'm doing great now. Thank you for just
sending a note and not coming to visit
like everyone else. It seemed like every
time I was about to get some rest,
another person whom I had to
entertain walked in."

A Gentleman and His Stationery

Since a gentleman may be called upon to write a note, extend an invitation, or dash off a few words of gratitude at any moment, he makes sure that he always has on hand a ready supply of writing paper and envelopes, note cards, good-quality pens, and postage.

The staples of his stationery stash will include supplies of

- **Monarch sheets** (writing paper measuring 7¼ by 10½ inches) in ecru, white, or pale gray. Monarch sheets, with their envelopes, may be used for personal or business correspondence. A gentleman may wish to have his name, along with his home address, engraved or printed at the top of each sheet. He will also want to have his address (without his name) added to the back flap of his envelopes.

- **Correspondence cards** (heavy-duty cards measuring 7¼ by 3⅞ inches) in ecru, white, or pale gray. Correspondence cards, which fit in the same envelopes as monarch sheets, may be used for almost any personal correspondence—sympathy notes, thank-you notes, and even party invitations. A gentleman may wish to have his name—without his address—engraved or printed on each card.

- **Enclosure cards** (heavy-duty cards measuring 3¼ by 1¾ inches) in ecru, white, or pale gray. Also known as "calling cards," enclosure cards come with their own envelopes and are engraved or printed with the gentleman's full name. These cards are too small to be mailed through the U.S. Postal Service. They are invaluable, however, when a gentleman needs to write a brief note to accompany a gift or when he simply wishes to jot down a quick message to be attached to a newspaper clipping, a photograph, or a photocopy of another document.

• **Postcards** in any number of colors and illustrated in all sorts of amusing and interesting ways. Simply by picking up a few attractive cards whenever he is in a gift shop or visiting a museum, a gentleman may accrue a collection of cards that he can use for any impromptu correspondence, including thank-you notes for gifts and informal get-togethers.

If a gentleman chooses to have his stationery engraved, he will be wise to go ahead and purchase his own solid brass "die," including his full name and his home address. The engraver can mask different portions of the die during the engraving process, so that the same die can serve for any of a gentleman's stationery needs.

Because high-quality stationery is not inexpensive, a gentleman may be well advised to write a draft of any note that he intends to send out on his personalized cards and papers.

INVITATIONS AND RESPONSES
TO THEM

When a gentleman invites friends, acquaintances, or coworkers to any occasion for which he is host, he makes sure he provides all the pertinent information in a clear, concise manner. He makes especially sure to include the time and location of the event, as well as some sort of explanation as to what sort of food and drink his guests may expect to find when they arrive. If he expects his guests to honor some sort of dress code, he makes sure it is clearly stipulated in his invitation. Even if he does not request that his guests "RSVP," he still includes a telephone number, since he knows that invariably somebody will need to call for directions.

A gentleman responds in a timely manner to any invitations he receives. Although most formal invitations include a response card, a gentleman should be able to compose an acceptance note if such a card is not included. For less formal occasions, a gentleman may either respond in writing or via phone. Responses to very casual invitations are expected to be, and are most appropriately, returned by phone.

When a gentleman accepts an invitation via note or phone, he makes sure to mention the date and time at which he is expected to arrive, just so his host (or hostess) knows that he understands the game plan; when he declines an invitation he need not reiterate the details, since he does not plan to be present.

An Invitation to a Somewhat Formal Occasion

[Printed on a computer or at a print shop, or handwritten on plain stationery or a sturdy correspondence card.]

Mitchell Mullins
requests the pleasure of your company for
Cocktails
7 o'clock
Friday, August 27
8746 Ocean Drive, Apt. 4-P
998-3313
Coat and tie

An Invitation to a Casual Get-together

Dear Millie,

I'm asking a few people over for drinks on Friday, July 27, at 7 o'clock. My friends Eddie and Abigail Jussworth will be in town for the weekend, and I want you to meet them.

We'll be very, very casual. I have a suspicion that Gil will be bringing his Twister game.

Please let me know if you can make it.

Looking forward to seeing you.

> All best,
> Mitch Mullins
> 998-3313

[Mitch will include his address on the outside of the envelope.]

A Gentleman Does Not Write:

"I will just be serving wine,
so if you want anything
stronger, BYOB."

THE MOST CASUAL INVITATION POSSIBLE
(OTHER THAN A PHONE CALL)

I'm pouring Cosmos on Friday.
Don't come before 7. Don't come after 10.
Call me.

Mitch
998-3313

A Response to a Formal Wedding Invitation

[Handwritten on plain stationery or a sturdy correspondence card.]

Jonathan Hazelbirth
is pleased to accept
Mrs. Needly's kind invitation for
Saturday, October 1
at the Overbought Club
following the ceremony at St. Ustley's Church

*[In this situation the gentleman is responding only to the invitation
to the reception, not to the wedding ceremony. The reception is the
social occasion. The wedding ceremony is a public church service
and therefore is theoretically open to the entire community. Also
note that a gentleman omits any punctuation at the line breaks.
The line breaks themselves take the place of the punctuation.]*

A Response Declining an Invitation to a Formal Wedding

Jonathan Hazelbirth
regrets that he is unable to accept
Mrs. Needly's kind invitation for
Saturday, October 1

A Written Response to a Somewhat Formal Invitation (such as Mitch Mullins's invitation for cocktails on page 77)

Dear Mitch,

Thanks for the invitation for 7 P.M. on Friday the 27th. I'll be there and I'm looking forward to it.

                              Thanks,
                              Gary

A Written Response Declining a Somewhat Formal Invitation
(such as Mitch Mullins's invitation for cocktails on page 77)

Dear Mitch,

I've received your invite for drinks on Friday the 27th. Unfortunately, I've already made plans to be in Gallville with my parents that weekend.

I know you'll have a great time. When I get back in town, I want to hear all about it.

Thanks so much for the invitation. I wish I could say yes.

Sincerely,
Gary

A Gentleman Does Not Write:

"I wish you had invited me earlier—before
I went and bought theater tickets for that evening."

When to Use Titles

In the excruciatingly correct correspondence of excruciatingly correct society, the name of any person—whether on the front of an envelope, or in the salutation of a letter—must be preceded by a title. "Honorific" titles such as "Mr.," "Ms.," "Miss," or "Mrs." are used merely as a matter of courtesy. "Professional" titles such as "Dr.," "Senator," or "Reverend" are used in business correspondence that actually relates to the title-holder's job, as well as in social correspondence.

A gentleman is never wrong in using an honorific or a professional title in his personal correspondence. However, he may choose whether to use a title based on his familiarity with the recipient and the formality of the correspondence. When a gentleman writes a thank-you note to his neighbor, who is a dentist and a close friend, he may address the envelope to "James Morton" and begin the letter "Dear James." However, when he sends this neighbor a formal wedding invitation, he addresses it to "Dr. James Morton."

A gentleman takes the time to consult an etiquette book or an appropriate Website to determine the correct form of address and salutation for any clergyman, government official, college or university official, member of the military, or other professional with whom he wishes to correspond. He may also find this information in the reference section of many dictionaries. He thus knows, when writing a congratulatory note to his senator, to address the envelope to "The Honorable Julia Ferrelli" and to begin his letter with the salutation "Dear Senator Ferrelli."

Mr., Miss, Ms., or Mrs.?

These days a gentleman is well warned to take care in applying honorific titles such as "Mr.," "Ms.," "Miss" or "Mrs." without foreknowledge. If he receives, for example, a letter signed by "Karey Thompson," he may find himself in a dilemma, unsure whether to reply to "Mr. Thompson" or "Ms. Thompson." His best bet in such cases is simply to reply to "Karey Thompson," both on his return envelope and in the salutation at the head of the enclosed letter or note.

While a gentleman may feel secure at almost any time in referring to women correspondents as "Ms. Smith," "Ms. Jones," or "Ms. Zilliwitsch," he is wise to defer to the implied wishes of a woman who has signed her letter—or even identified herself on the return envelope—as "Miss Zilliwitsch" or "Mrs. Patrick K. Magursky."

NOTES OF CONGRATULATION

A gentleman rejoices in the successes of his friends. Since such moments in life are invariably happy, he seizes upon them to offer his good wishes and joyous support. He knows that he will be with his friends during the hard times, but he also knows that his thoughtfulness is more than welcome in the good times too.

Even if his feelings regarding his friends' personal lives and accomplishments are not totally blissful, he knows that a note of congratulation is a little gift, not a chance to give a lecture. In such cases, if he feels that he cannot sincerely say he is happy with his friends' decisions, he is better off saying nothing at all. He knows, however, that whatever his personal standards or opinions, he does not impugn his own integrity by saying, "I wish you well."

A Note of Best Wishes upon an Engagement Announcement, Written to the Bride-to-Be

Dear Angela,

It was great to run into you and Bosco the other night and to hear your good news. If I may be so bold, I want it known that I've always said the two of you make a great couple.

You do know, don't you, that I met Bosco in junior high and that we've been great buddies ever since? I've told him over and over that great things were in store for him. Now I know my prediction has come true.

With all my best wishes,
Linus

A Gentleman Does Not Write:

"You snagged a good one."

A Note of Congratulation upon an Engagement Announcement, Written to the Groom-to-Be

Dear Bosco,

It made me happy to hear the great news about you and Angela. She is a wonderful woman. Good work, my friend.

I've told her how long we've known each other, but I didn't offer to tell her any tales from our days at Bixley High, especially the senior trip to D.C. That's the kind of real buddy I am.

I hope you know that you have my honest and heartfelt congratulations.

With all my best,
Linus

[In writing his note to Angela, Linus respects the tradition of offering his "best wishes" to the bride, while offering his "congratulations" to Bosco, the groom. The tradition stems from the idea that it is the man who is lucky to have won the woman. Linus would never think of congratulating Angela for having "snagged" Bosco.]

A Gentleman Does Not Write:

"Angela seems like a great catch, but I'd get a pre-nup just in case (ha ha)."

A Note of Best Wishes to a Newly Married Couple

Dear Maddie and Gilbert,

I saw the announcement of your wedding in today's *Examiner*. What good news that is. I'm passing a copy along to my mom, who will remember my talking about you when we worked together at the law firm.

Both of you are great folks. Please know that you have my warmest good wishes.

Sincerely,
Toby Marquess

A Gentleman Does Not Write:

"Sounds like it was a wonderful wedding.
Wish I had made the list."

A Note of Best Wishes to Be Enclosed with a Wedding Gift

Dear Maddie and Gilbert,

I hope these champagne flutes will play a part in the many celebrations that are to come as the two of you begin your life together.

With all my best wishes,
Jack Walburn

[Jack, of course, writes his quick, high-spirited note on a clean, heavyweight enclosure card. It may be solid white, ecru, or pale gray. If he has a stock of enclosure cards already engraved or printed with his full name, he simply signs his note "Jack," or he may, even more simply, just strike through his last name, "Wallburn," to make it clear that he considers himself to be on a first-name basis with the recipients. In no case would he use a business card for this absolutely social, and intimate, purpose.]

A Gentleman Does Not Write:

"If you don't like these, I got them
at Giard Gifts. You can return them."

A Note of Congratulation to a Lesbian or Gay Couple upon Their Commitment Ceremony

Dear Stacey and Jen,

It was such an honor for me to be present at your ceremony. It was a moving experience, not least of all because of the dignified, eloquent vows the two of you had penned.

And the reception was a pretty grand bash too. Nothing beats a good luau.

It was lovely to meet so many of your friends.

With sincere good wishes,
Angus

A Gentleman Does Not Write:

"You two deserve to be married for real."

A Note of Congratulation upon the Birth of a Baby

Dear Ros and Mike,

I just heard the wonderful news that little Roslyn Michelle has arrived. I know the two of you must be exhausted, but I bet you can't tell whether it's from sleep deprivation or from sheer joy and the anticipation of all the great adventures that lie ahead of you and your little girl.

I want to be introduced to her sometime before too long, just as I look forward to congratulating the two of you in person.

All my best,
Flaven

A Gentleman Does Not Write:

"I can't wait to meet the little girl
who made Mike miss so many poker
games on Lamaze class nights."

A Note of Congratulation upon a Milestone Anniversary

Dear Whitney and Wally,

I read in the newspaper about the celebration of your forty years together. When I look at the two of you, I get a sense of how wonderful those years, and decades, have been. I am also proud to be able to have shared some of those good times in the warmth of your beautiful home.

You are excellent role models for all of us, as you continue to contribute so much to making the world a better place.

It is my great honor, and pleasure, to be your friend.

Please know that you have my sincere congratulations and my warmest best wishes.

Joy to both of you,
Zack Moberton

A Gentleman Does Not Write:

"Congrats on sticking it out this long. I know
from my own experience that it isn't easy."

A Note of Congratulation upon a Friend's New Job

Dear Alex,

I hear you're starting at Douster & Sons next week. I know the company's reputation and understand that the people there are great folks.

They're also very smart if they've got the good sense to hire you.

Let's get together for lunch sometime, now that you're going to be working downtown.

Congratulations to you, and to the Dousters.

Sincerely,
Rick

A Gentleman Does Not Write:

"Now that you're making the big bucks,
lunch is on you."

A Note of Congratulation upon a Friend's or Coworker's Retirement

Dear Eleanor,

On my very first day at the office, you were the very first person to offer a word of welcome. Actually, I don't exactly remember it being a "welcome." What I do remember you saying was, "May I show you how to make the coffee?"

That's the kind of practical knowledge you've continued to impart year in and year out. I remain so grateful for your counsel and camaraderie over the years.

Congratulations on your retirement, even though I'm missing you already.

Sincerely,
Nate

A Gentleman Does Not Write:

"Expect some calls from me asking you questions—you are the only one who knows how to do the quarterly report."

A Note of Congratulation upon the Recent Success of a Friend or Acquaintance

Dear Bono,

I saw your new CD in Disc-a-Thon yesterday. Frankly, I couldn't miss it, considering the size of the display.

When I took my copy to the register, three other people in line were buying copies too. That's the best news possible, I guess.

Isn't it great to see your hard work pay off? I look forward to saying, "I knew him when." In fact, I'm saying it already.

I'll be watching for you on the awards shows.

All my best,
Roger

A Gentleman Does Not Write:

"I hope being a star will
be everything you hoped
it would be."

How to Address an Envelope

When addressing an envelope, a gentleman's main goal is to make sure that his message reaches its recipient as expeditiously as possible. He attempts to write clearly, providing up-to-date address details and including his recipient's postal code—in *every* case. (In the United States, the five-digit zip code is obligatory, but a gentleman knows that adding the "plus four" code may help ensure that his mail reaches its destination more smoothly.)

In social correspondence, the first line of a standard address includes the name of the recipient or recipients of the letter, along with any appropriate social or professional titles. The second line includes the street address, including any relevant apartment or suite number. The third line includes the city, state, and postal code to which the envelope is to be delivered. For example:

> Mr. and Mrs. Joseph Grant
> 226 Gustavus Lane, Apartment A-6
> Nashville, TN 37205-3932

The U.S. Postal Service requests that standard two-letter abbreviations be used for the fifty states (for example, "ME" for Maine or "WY" for Wyoming). However, a gentleman may choose to either spell out or abbreviate other standard elements of the address, according to his preference. He may use "Street" or "St.," "Avenue" or "Ave.," trusting that—if his penmanship is proficient—his envelope will reach its recipient in a timely manner.

If a gentleman has *any* reason to assume that his correspondence may be returned to him (or if he simply wants to make sure that his correspondent has the right information for getting in touch with him), he makes sure that his return address is included on any envelope he puts in the mail. He may choose to place his return address on the upper left-hand corner of the *front* of the envelope. Or he may place it on the flap on the *back* of the envelope. Either way he is correct. What is more, if an envelope must be returned, the Postal Service employees are trained to look in *either* spot for the sender's address.

Notes of Apology and Responses to Them

A gentleman makes every effort to behave himself at all times and hopes never to give distress or displeasure to another person. Yet he remains—for all his good intentions—a fallible human being, which means that from time to time, and on what he hopes are infrequent occasions, he does screw up.

Because he is a gentleman, however, he attempts to straighten out the situation (and recoup his losses) as quickly as possible. He knows that, in most cases, apologies are best offered in person, or at least by telephone, since face-to-face communication may actually help calm the waters more easily. It may even give him a better insight into his affronted friend's side of the story.

If his friend or acquaintance is convinced that he or she

has been severely insulted or that the gentleman has been intentionally rude or thoughtless, the gentleman may even be accused of cowardice for apologizing in writing. Nevertheless, some situations demand that a gentleman attempt to make amends by means of the written word.

Even if a gentleman feels that he has been misinterpreted or wrongly accused, he may find it noble to say, "I am sorry that my actions caused you unhappiness [or even "pain"]. I hope you know that I did not mean to give offense." He never turns an apology into an argument on his own behalf or a defense of his own behavior.

The only time a gentleman may correctly refuse to offer an apology is when he has been accused of rudeness when standing up for his ethical convictions or his political beliefs. Even then, however, if he has raised his voice to the point of bullying or if he has disrupted a dinner party by provoking an argument at the table, he may still find it necessary to say, "I'm sorry for letting my anger get the best of me."

Knowing how to say "I'm sorry" is a valued skill, but it is not one that a gentleman wishes to hone by overuse. A gentleman is well advised to attempt at all times to live his life in a way that requires as few apologies as possible.

If a gentleman receives an apology in the form of a note, he must respond to that gesture in a timely manner. A note of acceptance of an apology should simply say the offending party is forgiven, so that life may get back to normal. A gentleman does not wait, hoping that he will run into Grace at a cocktail party where he can tell her he accepts her apology. He may not run into Grace anytime soon; more important, he would never open an old wound, especially in the midst of a happy occasion.

An Apology Note After Destroying a Piece of a Host's Heirloom China (or Any Other Valued Property)

Dear Agatha,

You were kind to be so gracious about my clumsiness at your wonderful dinner party on Saturday evening. I wish I had noticed the casserole coming across the table, but I didn't.

I hope you'll forgive me for being such an oaf.

Sincerely,
Percy

[In such situations, a gentleman never offers to pay for replacing the damaged property (not only because he does not know what sort of financial commitment he may be making but also because the damaged goods may truly be irreplaceable). He may, however, actually find a way to replace a shattered wineglass or a broken dinner plate. If he can accomplish such a feat, he can be confident of having provided restitution in full.]

A Gentleman Does Not Write:

"Please accept this check for forty dollars for
the salad plate I broke—I checked on
eBay and that should cover it."

An Apology Note for
Inappropriate Behavior

Dear Doris,

I realize now that I behaved rather badly at the reception following little Kaitlyn's christening. The truth of the matter is, I had way too much of the celebratory champagne. I hope you know that otherwise I would never have attempted to wear Kaitlyn's car seat on my head.

This was a day that should evoke only good memories in the future. Please forgive me if my behavior has marred those memories in any way.

Sincerely,
Randy

A Gentleman Does Not Write:

"If it makes you feel any better,
I had the world's worst hangover
the next morning."

An Apology Note for Having Missed a Business Appointment

Dear Mr. Grousehawk:

Please accept my apology for having missed our lunch appointment yesterday. After having been caught for more than an hour in the traffic jam caused by an accident on the highway, I did finally manage to get in touch with your assistant, Ms. Tidwell, who told me your schedule had required that you proceed without me.

I understand the demands of your schedule, and I wish I could have alerted you sooner. I hope we will be able to reschedule a time to get together, and I still look forward to sharing my proposal with you.

Sincerely,
Malcolm Habbyway

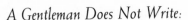

A Gentleman Does Not Write:

"Sorry about missing the appointment,
but something came up that I couldn't get
out of. I'm sure you understand."

An Apology Note for Having Missed a Social Occasion

Dear Enrique,

I'm so sorry to have missed last night's dinner party. I was looking forward to it, and I was especially excited about having the chance to see Stephanie again.

Unfortunately, late in the afternoon I was hit with a twenty-four-hour bug of some sort. I'm only getting back up to speed right now, and it's 5 o'clock on Sunday.

I know the dinner was great. I regret having to miss a good time with so many great folks.

Sincerely,
Hiram

A Gentleman Does Not Write:

"I'm sorry I missed the party,
but if I had been there I would have
been upchucking all
over the place."

An Apology Note to a Friend Who Feels He Has Been Insulted

Dear Arthur,

I fear that I hurt your feelings on Saturday evening when I mentioned your new hairpiece in front of the Leskies. It was not my intention to cause you any embarrassment or discomfort, and I realize now that I should have been more careful about making this sort of remark in front of anyone—especially people with whom you are not well acquainted.

I consider you a good friend, and I am sorry for having put you, and the Leskies, on the spot.

Please accept my sincere apology.

Yours truly,
Bill

A Gentleman Does Not Write:

"Sorry about the hairpiece remark.
I always seem to put my foot in my mouth
in awkward situations."

A Response to an Apology

Dear Bill,

Thank you for your note. You were good to send it.

I have to admit that the "new rug" remark did catch me a bit off guard, but I fully understand that you meant no harm. You are a friend and a person well known for his thoughtfulness and consideration for others.

I appreciate your writing. It has completely cleared the air, as far I'm concerned.

Sincerely,
Arthur

A Gentleman Does Not Write:

"I accept your apology.
Just don't let it happen again."